Reflections for the Effective Nonprofit Donor

A volume of the Effective Philanthropy and
Fund Raising series.

Reflections for the Effective Nonprofit Donor

Quotes, axioms and observations to help you fund our important institutions

Jim Norvell

Writers Club Press

San Jose   New York   Lincoln   Shanghai

Reflections for the Effective Nonprofit Donor
Quotes, axioms and observations to help
you fund our important institutions

Writers Club Press
an imprint of iUniverse, Inc.

For information address:
iUniverse, Inc.
5220 S. 16th St., Suite 200
Lincoln, NE 68512
www.iuniverse.com

Artistic license was exercised with the quotes borrowed from an illustrious array of thoughtful people. Insertion of their observations in juxtaposition to my own was based on their unique similarity, often taken out of context. Those who are still around to do so are free to do the same with mine.

ISBN: 0-595-20879-7

Printed in the United States of America

For those who care

This book is dedicated to the millions of compassionate and generous people around the world who knew long before September 11, 2001 that humanity is a fragile web. They have recognized our total interdependence and selflessly shared personal resources for the common good. One of the most moving statements I have ever heard was from a young woman whose generosity is out of proportion to her means. She said, "When I decided that charity was an important part of my life, I knew that it would have little meaning if I gave only what is comfortable. Since the moment I made that commitment, my life has been rewarded ten times over. The more I give, the more I get in return." To her. To all of you.

It is another's fault if he be ungrateful; but it is mine if I do not give. To find one thankful man, I will oblige a great many that are not so. I had rather never receive a kindness than never bestow one. Not to return a benefit is a great sin; but not to confer one is a greater.

Seneca

A Sermon to the Choir

Cicero said, *"Men resemble the gods in nothing so much as in doing good to their fellow creatures."* While his intent was to elevate generosity to lofty stature, his statement hints that we may perform those good deeds sometimes to achieve god-like stature. In that short quote from the 1st Century BC is the conundrum that plagues philanthropy to this day—where is the dividing line past which a gift is given more for what it does for the donor than what it can do for the recipient? And, is that important?

I'll give you two takes on the question from my experience and observation.

First take. As a fundraiser, I want the most powerful motivation I can find to influence you to give. If I know what gives you satisfaction - if I can fill a need within you - I want to know it. I don't care whether you are really committed to the organization because once you make an investment in it, you will probably confirm that decision with subsequent investments. If you are not adherents and advocates from the beginning, over time you may become both. If I have satisfied a big enough need and I can continue to reinforce that satisfaction, you will give even more generously over time. If you do give at significant levels, I want that fact known so it becomes an example for the solicitation of others.

For those reasons, I want to elevate you to god-like status.

Second take. From observing thousands of significant donors' behavior, there seems to be an inverse relationship between obvious donor benefit and deep donor satisfaction. I have always experienced the most joy from giving when it was relatively unprompted and without public notice. Donors who are very generous, even proactive in their giving, tend to be uncomfortable with gushing gestures of gratitude. The most sophisticated of you do allow various forms of public recognition, though, because you know it is helpful in soliciting others, but you want to make sure that sufficient acclaim is still left for those who may require it. You receive tasteful gift acknowledgments gracefully, because you know it is important for the recipients to develop a culture of gratitude, not entitlement.

For those reasons, most of you avoid being elevated to god-like status.

Generosity is a gift from God. Those who exhibit it are the hands of God on earth. Thank you for your gracious support of important organizations and causes.

Jim Norvell

Quotes, axioms and observations to help you fund our important institutions

This book was compiled as a resource for nonprofit donors. It contains key guidelines I have found to be useful in judging the performance of nonprofit organizations. Finally, I wrote it because I like quotes and have found that many of you share that enjoyment.

The inequities of life demand philanthropy.

We must build a new world, a far better world—one in which the eternal dignity of man is respected.

Harry S. Truman

Social consciousness is the first step in a philanthropic solution.

We must have the press of the crowd to draw virtue from us.

Angelo Patri

If the gift does not affect the donor's life, it is merely a handout—not philanthropy.

Do not be conformed to this world, but be transformed.

Romans 12:2 (NRSV)

Philanthropy is created by the same drives that fuel competition.

All of our dreams can come true—if we have the courage to pursue them.

Walt Disney

Most philanthropy is based on emotion.

Emotion has taught mankind to reason.

Marquis de Vauvenargues

Philanthropy is the socialism of democracy.

Whoever has two coats must share with anyone who has none; and whoever has food must do likewise.

Luke 3:11 (NRSV)

The more social freedom we experience,
the greater our need for philanthropy.

I believe we are here on planet earth to live, grow up, and do what we can to make this world a better place for all people to enjoy freedom.

Rosa Parks

Philanthropy is second only to the vote in embodying democracy.

Money spent on ourselves may be a millstone around the neck; spent on others it may give us wings like eagles.

Roswell Dwight Hitchcock

Philanthropy alone cannot bridge all
social inequities, but, with government as
an ally and enabler, it can minimize them.

Giving away a fortune is taking Christianity too far.

Charlotte Bingham

The quality of life in the United States would be unexceptional without philanthropy.

If there is one word that describes our form of society in America, it may be the word—voluntary.

Lyndon Baines Johnson

Philanthropy is a quid pro quo transaction.

As the purse is emptied, the heart is filled.

Victor Hugo

Altruism is more likely to appear as instinctual heroism than as charity.

There are two perfectly good men; one dead and the other yet unborn.

Chinese proverb

Jim Norvell

A philanthropic transaction is a valuation and an exchange.

Decide what you want, decide what you are willing to exchange for it. Establish your priorities and go to work.

H. L. Hunt

Self interest regulates all transactions, philanthropy included.

A man does not have to be an angel
to be a saint.

Albert Schweitzer

The philanthropic exchange is not always apparent.

A bone to the dog is not charity. Charity is the bone shared with the dog, when you are just as hungry as the dog.

Jack London

Negotiation is common in major philanthropic transactions.

Let every eye negotiate for itself
And trust no agent.

William Shakespeare

The apparent motivation for
generosity may be misleading.

Take egotism out and you would castrate the benefactors.

Ralph Waldo Emerson

Altruism is highly overrated.

Every major horror in history was committed in the name of an altruistic motive.

Ayn Rand

The Philanthropic Sector is a response to life's inequities and the need to serve.

Life has no meaning except in terms of responsibility.

Reinhold Niebuhr

Social consciousness is at the root of philanthropy.

We will have to repent in this generation not merely for the vitriolic words and actions of bad people, but for the appalling silence of the good people.

Martin Luther King, Jr.

Philanthropic acts stem from
resonance between the needs of
others and personal value systems.

*Many organizations are very clear about
the needs they would like to serve, but they
don't understand these needs from the
perspective of the customers.*

Philip Kotler

Philanthropy is a gift on one side and a promise on the other.

A mind conscious of integrity scorns to say more than it means to perform.

Robert Burns

Everyone has needs that philanthropy meets.

Trouble is a part of your life, and if you don't share it, you don't give the person who loves you enough chance to love you enough.

Dinah Shore

Nonprofit privilege and huge revenue stream make philanthropy an inviting target for government control.

Worry about the motives of those who worry about the motives of the charitable, since they may use this [excuse] to bolster their own political attitudes or comfort themselves with their own miserliness.

Benedict Nightingale

Too often, philanthropy is marketed only through fund raising.

I get fifteen or twenty letters a day for everything from Yugoslavian dog illnesses to marathon diseases. It numbs you.... So you write off a check for twenty dollars to a charity to absolve yourself of guilt.

Anjelica Huston

Philanthropy is both a behavior and an ideal.

Be not merely good; be good for something.

Henry David Thoreau

We have an inherent need to reinforce personal values.

The poor don't know that their function in life is to exercise our generosity.

Jean Paul Sartre

People have difficulty reconciling
philanthropic ideals with the very
practical process of fund raising.

Words without actions are the assassin of idealism.

Herbert Hoover

Generosity is based upon financial realities, shifting competitive interests and a sub-conscious value system.

It is not how much we give, but how much love we put into the giving.

Mother Teresa

Fund raising is a term used for a variety of activities, not all philanthropic.

A cowl does not a monk make.

Medieval Proverb

Good fund raising maximizes gains and minimizes losses for both the donor and the organization.

Hope of ill gain is the beginning of loss.

Democritus

Good fund raising is done with dignity and without apology.

To keep a lamp burning, we have to keep putting oil in it.

Mother Teresa

Showing prospects the importance of their gifts allows them to make the organization their own.

I suspect people of plotting to make me happy.

J. D. Salinger

Fund-raising planning must include key members of the top donor prospect constituencies.

Any clever person can make plans for winning a war if he has no responsibility for carrying them out.

Winston Spencer Churchill

Fund raising relies on resonating values, powerful influences, peer-level solicitation and the desire for rewarding affiliation.

As for the largest-hearted of us, what is the word we write most often in our chequebooks? — "Self."

Eden Phillpotts

Individuals give 90% of the money
donated to philanthropic causes.

You cannot ask us to take sides against arithmetic.

Winston Spencer Churchill

Lower income and upper income donors out give the middle income donor.

The middle class is always a firm champion of equality when it concerns the class above it; but it is always its inveterate foe when it concerns the class below it.

Orestes A. Brownson

Religious and human service organizations largely rely on the generosity of the average citizen.

I have to live for others and not myself;
that's middle class morality.

George Bernard Shaw

Trying to elicit a uniform response from
all donors invites failure.

If you seek average gifts, you get below-average results.

James Gregory Lord

Donor recognition reinforces personal values and maximizes both response and loyalty.

Praise shames me, for I secretly beg for it.

Rabindranath Tagore

Appreciation is the least expensive and most effective form of cultivation.

The average man is more interested in a woman who is interested in him than he is in a woman with beautiful legs.

Marlene Dietrich

Effective fund raising creates a *sense of involvement* when real involvement is not possible.

Illusions are art, for the feeling person, and it is by art that we live, if we do.

Elizabeth Bowen

Ordinary events for the ordinary
organization are a very inefficient way to
raise money.

Idealism is fine, but as it approaches reality the cost becomes prohibitive.

William F. Buckley, Jr.

The hardest gift to get is one from a former donor discouraged by apparent ingratitude.

Gratitude is merely the secret hope of future favors.

Francois de la Rochefoucald

Designated gifts allow the donor to
personalize his or her support.

In baiting a mousetrap with cheese, always leave a little room for the mouse.

Saki

Major gift programs are built on donor satisfaction.

Here is a simple but powerful rule...always give people more than they expect to get.

Nelson Boswell

The most basic fund-raising hope is that the chair will be the major donor.

By working faithfully eight hours a day, you may eventually get to be a boss and work twelve hours a day.

Robert Frost

Planned giving offers constituents
financial planning benefits, so it is not
just a solicitation, but a service.

Property is intended to serve life.

Martin Luther King, Jr.

The greatest fund-raising success is, even while being savored, nothing more than duty realized.

The best preparation for the future is the present well seen to, the last duty well done.

George Macdonald

Donors satisfy value-driven needs when they provide philanthropic support.

I have found that the best way to give advice to your children is to find out what they want and then advise them to do it.

Harry S. Truman

We have an inherent need to
reinforce personal values.

The poor don't know that their function in life is to exercise our generosity.

Jean Paul Sartre

Need is the perception of deficiency and the opportunity to approach fulfillment.

A poor person who is unhappy is in a better position than a rich person who is unhappy. Because the poor person has hope. He thinks money would help.

Jean Kerr

Everything is a value judgment.

Values are the lens through which self sees the world.

Tom Reynolds

Values are not static, but changes are few and far between.

All change is not growth; all movement is not forward.

Ellen Glasgow

People differentiate nonprofits by evaluating them against their personal value systems.

Caring is personal. It is rooted in an individual's own set of values, concerns and aspirations.

Peter M. Senge

Instinctual response and the conditioning
of experience shape human behavior.

Men are wise in proportion, not to their experience, but to their capacity for experience.

George Bernard Shaw

Personal needs are an effort to
shape reality.

Reality is something that you rise above.

Liza Minnelli

Life is defined by the drive to fulfill personal needs.

The significance of man is not what he attains but rather what he hopes to attain.

Kahlil Gibran

Values evolve to regulate needs.

It's not hard to make decisions when you know what your values are.

Roy Disney

Individual values regulate decision-making processes.

Why does a man act as he does? What would be required for a man to act differently? The key to motivation lies in the realm of values.

Nathaniel Brandon

Choices reflect and reinforce deeply-held values.

We don't see things as they are, we see them as we are.

Anaïs Nin

We are uniquely defined by the way we express our values.

A man is literally what he thinks.

James Allen

The perceived consequences of behavior are balanced against personal goals.

You can do anything in the world if you are prepared to take the consequences.

W. Somerset Maugham

Understanding group values increases likelihood of developing linkages.

Public opinion is a thermometer a monarch should constantly consult.

Napoleon I

We reveal our values when we tell others
what is important to us.

Friends are my heart and my ears.

Michael Jordan

Nonprofits should periodically research constituent values to understand the "mind of the market."

Grace is given of God, but knowledge is bought in the market.

Arthur Hugh Clough

Gifts reflect the donor's needs.

Nobody has ever measured, even poets, how much the heart can hold.

Zelda Fitzgerald

Donors satisfy value-driven needs when they provide philanthropic support.

I have found that the best way to give advice to your children is to find out what they want and then advise them to do it.

Harry S. Truman

Donors have rights that organizations should look upon as obligations.

There's no such thing as a free lunch.

Milton Friedman

Situational ethics aren't ethical.

I think its better to come in second than to be impeached.

George McGovern

Character is the expression ethical standards.

In matters of style, swim with the current;
in matters of principle, stand like a rock.

Thomas Jefferson

Commitment to ethical standards defines organizations and people.

If ever I said, in grief or pride,
I tired of honest things, I lied.

Edna St.Vincent Millay

Influential leaders shape the organizational culture.

The manager administers, the leader innovates. The manager maintains, the leader develops. The manager relies on systems, the leader relies on people. ...The manager does things right, the leader does the right things.

Forbes Magazine

Nonprofits must abide by ethical standards in a much more public way than private sector organizations.

Many people like to believe charities as dishonest as they are supposedly mismanaged. They actually prefer them that way, because it means that they do not have to feel guilty about their own lack of generosity.

Benedict Nightingale

Fund raising's fiduciary implications demand specific ethical standards of the highest magnitude.

The knights had to vow poverty, chastity, and obedience. They only kept the last vow.

Gen. George S. Patton, Jr.

Ethics are a contract between the organization and its constituents.

I only know that what is moral is what you feel good after and what is immoral is what you feel bad after.

Ernest Hemingway

Ethical conduct is influenced, but not guaranteed by standards.

My best friend is the one who brings out the best in me.

Henry Ford

The highest ideals demand the highest standards of conduct.

The ultimate test for us of what truth means is the conduct it dictates or inspires.

William James

About the Author

James R. (Jim) Norvell

Jim is a second-generation fundraiser who began his career immediately after graduating from Southern Illinois University–Edwardsville. He served in annual fund positions at Monticello College, the Foundation for Independent Colleges of Pennsylvania and Washington University before joining G. A. Brakeley & Co., Inc., Los Angeles, as a capital fundraiser. He left Brakeley to form his own capital campaign consulting firm, Development Management Associates, Inc. (DMA) and to earn his MBA at UCLA. Over fifteen years, he and partner Bob Zuer expanded DMA to $2 million in annual billings, serving clients throughout the Western United States, Great Britain and Australia.

0-595-20879-7

www.ingramcontent.com/pod-product-compliance
Lightning Source LLC
Chambersburg PA
CBHW031054180526
45163CB00002BA/825